KIDS BEDTIME SLEEP MEDITATIONS

Guided Night Time Short Stories And Positive Affirmations To Help Children & Toddlers Fall Asleep At Night, Relax, And Have Beautiful Dreams

Author: Sleepy Willow

Copyright 2021 – All rights reserved.

The content contained within this book may not be reproduced, duplicated or transmitted without direct written permission from the author or the publisher.

Under no circumstances will any blame or legal responsibility be held against the publisher, or author, for any damages, reparation, or monetary loss due to the information contained within this book. Either directly or indirectly.

Legal Notice:

This book is copyright protected.

This book is only for personal use. You cannot amend, distribute, sell, use, quote or paraphrase any part, or content within this book, without the consent of the author or publisher.

Disclaimer Notice:

Please not the information contained within this document is for educational and entertainment purposes only.

No warranties of any kind are declared or implied. Readers acknowledge that the author is not engaging in the rendering of legal, financial, medical or professional advice.

The content within this book has been derived from various sources. Please consult a licensed professional before attempting any techniques outlined in this book.

By reading this document, the reader agrees that under no circumstances is the author responsible for any losses, direct or indirect, which are incurred as a result of the use of the information contained within this document, including, but not limited to: errors, omissions, or inaccuracies.

Table of content

Introduction 1

Chapter 1 3
   The Ancient Story Book 3

Chapter 2 13
   Enchanted Treehouse 13

Chapter 3 22
   Pirate Adventure 22

Chapter 4 38
   Wishing Waterfall 38

Chapter 5 48
   Ancient Mountains 48

Chapter 6 57
   African Safari Adventure 57

Chapter 7 65
   Magic Crystal Island 65

Chapter 8 72
   Koala Grove 72

Chapter 9 80
   Wolf Guardian 80

Chapter 10	89
Puppy Kingdom	89
Chapter 11	98
Owl Spirit	98
Chapter 12	105
Limiting Belief Buster	105
Conclusion	146

INTRODUCTION

Thank you for listening and choosing *Kids Bedtime Sleep Meditations.*

In this magical and wonderful book, you will be taken on many adventures and listen to wonderful stories that will help you to fall asleep peacefully every night. I hope that you and your children will have hours of fun listening to these stories. Each story in this book will be entertaining and will have small lessons that your child can learn from. You will learn many skills that can help you relax your mind and body, so you have the most amazing sleep every night. Each story contains valuable lessons while relieving stress. Each story will empower you and your children to improve your self-confidence and self-esteem. You will learn how to deal with your emotions better and communicate them more effectively.

Children who experience lots of nightmares might be scared to fall asleep at night and might have a hard time relaxing at night because they are afraid of scary dreams. This book will help you combat and get rid of those fears. Each story will help you feel more relaxed, calm, loved, and completely safe. You have nothing to worry about from now on.

After you have brushed your teeth, combed your hair, and put on nice comfortable pajamas, it's time for you to snuggle down in bed and get ready for sleep. You can now pick any story to help you relax and drift off to an amazing sleep.

Make sure you listen to each story and follow along. Each story has a relaxing meditation to help you get cozy and comfortable for a good night's sleep.

Are you ready to begin your bedtime meditation stories? Choose any story to begin your adventure now!

CHAPTER 1

The Ancient Story Book

Welcome to this part of the book, which is a guided sleep meditation.

This is where you will discover the enchanted and mysterious storybook.

Are you ready for this adventure using your incredible and wonderful imagination?

You will embark a journey to the peaceful ancient forest.

This is where the magical storybook is waiting for you.

If you are now ready to discover this magical and enchanted storybook's secret hiding place, then I want you to close your eyes now.

Make sure your body is comfortable and snug for you to relax deeply.

Remember that only all of the meditation magic happens in that dreamy state of being almost awake and almost asleep.

Now imagine you are at the countryside with your family.
You are staying in a log cabin on the edge of an ancient and wise forest.
Now imagine you are standing outside your cabin in the garden, looking at all of the tall trees.
Imagine how peaceful it is here.
You now quickly feel the fresh earthy air on your face.
You now easily smell the fresh smell of wildflowers and grass.
You hear the happy chirping and singing of birds and the humming bees buzzing along.

The breeze of the wind is so gentle against your skin.
You feel the warmth of sunshine upon your face.
The sunlight is bright and glows all around you.
It is like a glorious force field.
Take some deep breaths in and out.

You are now feeling so relaxed.

You are now feeling so connected to the land and to the healthy and earthy energies of nature.

You start walking past the flower bed and past the vegetable patch.

At the very end of the garden, you push open the wooden gate and close it behind you.

A wave of freedom and excitement washes all over you.

The forest seems to be inviting you to explore it further.

You follow the green grass path that winds through the trees.

The grass feels so soft and fluffy underneath you as you follow this twisting path.

You look around, and you see to your amazement that some of the trees have old and wise faces on their ancient tree trunks.

It looks as if these giant trees are smiling with happiness, wisdom, and making silly faces at you as you walk past them.

You smile back happily at their funny and kind faces as you walk past these trees.

You notice now that the old trees are looking in all different directions with their eyes.

They are pointing the way along the path by looking in different directions.

You allow these ancient wise old trees to guide you as you follow the ways their eyes are pointing.

They are leading you down a winding path deeper and deeper into the forest.

You trust the wisdom of these trees and they are showing you the hidden way.

You wonder what you will discover as you follow the secret way of the trees.

You have now arrived at a massive, gigantic oak tree.

It is the biggest and tallest tree you have ever seen.

It is utterly beautiful and magnificent.

This oak tree is so thick and all of the branches spread upwards and outwards.

Expanding so wide and all the way up to the tip tops of the forests.

The oak tree has the wisest and kindest old face on its trunk.

It kind of reminds you of an old and ancient wizard.

You now notice the trunk is hollow and has a natural space big enough to climb into, but it is really close to the ground.

The massive oak tree smiles down at you, and you sense it is inviting you to explore the inside of the tree.

You are feeling very excited and very curious.

You climb up and into the hollow tree.

Inside it is like a wooden cave.

It looks quite mysterious and surprisingly cozy.

In the middle of the tree is a small table and has a big brown leather book on top of the table.

You now take a closer look.

The cover of the book has lots of pictures of strange and magical creatures.

There are also symbols you do not recognize etched into the book.

The book is painted with what looks like real gold.

The edges of the book looks very old.

It could be from ancient times in history.

You can tell that this book is not modern at all.
It looks like it is handmade by an ancient artist.
You slowly reach your hand out and run your fingers along the pictures and symbols that are so precisely carved into the cover of the book.
The illustrations on the cover are of dragons, unicorns, lions, and every other magical creature you can ever imagine.
With a deep breath, now you decide to open the book.
You open the book and touch the pictures of all the celebrations in the book.
You also look at ancient maps of different and strange lands.
The book is so heavy, and a puff of golden dust glows and sparkles from the book all around you.
Wow, this is amazing.
This gold dust starts to swirl around and dazzle you. Little spirals of light dance and glow up from the pages.
To your surprise, as you look through this ancient book, you see it contains many myths, fairy tales, and legends told from long ago.
Even some of your favorite stories of all time are in this book, waiting just for you.

The illustrations from this book are some of the most beautiful and unique paintings you have ever seen.

The painting is so detailed.

The writing of the book was handwritten in a lovely script font in black ink.

Now suddenly, the golden magical energy that dazzled you and your whole body now starts to shrink you.

You shrink down and down.

Smaller and smaller.

You are now absolutely tiny!

You are now standing on the pages of the book.

All of these pictures suddenly spring up into 3d all around you.

The pages of the book have come to life.

All of the characters in the book wave, welcome you, and start talking to you.

Wow, this is so amazing!

Now you realize and understand you can be whatever character you want in the story.

You can be the hero of the story and the most important character in the story if you wish.

Wow, this is so much fun.

Any story that you can possibly imagine is right here in this book, waiting just for you.

Whatever fairytale you want or a storyland that is enchanted is waiting for you to explore it.

The storybook will take you there instantly.

You feel so alive and happy.

Wow, this is such an amazing and exciting adventure.

What story do you want to be apart of now?

What character would you love to meet and possibly maybe go on an adventure with?

What character would you like to be?

Spend some time now to just look at the book and just turn the pages.

The magical pages.

You get to pick and enjoy being a character in any story that you wish.

When you hear my voice return, it will then be time for you to dream off into the most happiest and deepest dreams.

Have some fun, and I will be with you again soon.

After you have spent some time having the most wonderful and amazing time turning the ancient book pages and living in the fairy tale storylands, it is now time for you to return back home.

Wave goodbye to all the characters in this magical, enchanting book.

All of the characters now wave back to you, and a sparkle of golden dust shimmers all around you.

You now start to grow bigger and bigger and bigger until you are once again your normal size.

You now close the magical storybook with both of your hands.

You now thank the storybook for the fun adventure.

You wonder who wrote the book, and you wonder who illustrated all of the pictures.

Well, I guess it will forever remain a mystery.

You climb out of the hidden hollow space of the ancient wise old oak tree.

You give the tree a great big hug.

The old wise old face smiles at you with happiness and wisdom.

Now you see that the oak tree's eyes look towards the way back home.

As you walk past the wise, kind trees, their eyes point and lead you in the direction you need to go through the forest.

Their wise old faces lead the way smiling down at you and helping you get back home.

When you arrive back at the log cabin, you climb into your warm and cozy bed.
You feel the warm covers all around you.
You feel so safe, loved, and amazingly happy as you just drift off to sleep deeply now.
You have a sense of fun and freedom that fills your heart as you drift off into the most beautiful dreams.
You know in your heart that the enchanted storybook is waiting just for you to return.
The magical enchanted book is always going to be there resting on the little table in the ancient wise old oak tree for you to read and enjoy anytime you wish.
Sweet ancient old enchanted storybook dreams.

29 minutes

CHAPTER 2

Enchanted Treehouse

Now welcome to a dreamy sleep meditation.

This is where you will discover the most fantastic and magnificent tree house hidden deep within an ancient forest.

This special treehouse is waiting just for you.

Now just close your eyes, and let's begin our journey.

Remember the meditation magic can only happen in the sleepy place where you are almost awake and almost asleep.

Now get really comfortable.

Take a big deep breath in and a long breath out.

That's wonderful.

Again take a deep breath in all the way down to your belly and then a calm breath out.

Now your body will keep breathing like this all by itself as your whole body relaxes now.
Your eyes and mouth are now fully relaxed.
Your belly is totally relaxed and free.
Your arms and legs are feeling very heavy now.
Even your hands and feet are relaxing now too.
That's fantastic.
Well done.

Now imagine you are standing in a beautiful forest.
The trees are tall and wise.
These trees also have fairy lanterns and fireflies all hanging around their branches.
The grass feels oh so soft and fluffy underneath your feet.
The moonlight is shining down between the trees making the entire forest glow.
You feel and sense this is a magical and enchanted place.
The starlight sparkles down over you and all-around your body.
You are now shining like a bright star too.
You are feeling so safe, loved, and calm in this forest.

You now notice a path made up of the moonlight shining the way between the trees.

You start to walk along this path now following the silvery moonlight.

It twist, turns, and winds through the forest as it leads you deeper and deeper into the ancient forest.

You walk along a stream of water that is bubbling along.

The silvery moonlight is shining down.

You can see pixies and fairies flying and darting about.

They are dancing on lily pads and on rocks.

They are playing by the babbling brook and maybe even going for a dip and having a swim.

They all smile and wave to you as you walk by them.

This path continues to lead you alongside a crystal clear stream.

You now breathe in and notice the air is so healthy, damp and you can smell the fresh scent of lavender flowers.

The grass is soft and tickles your bare feet very gently.

The moonlit path stops now, and it circles around the oldest tree in the ancient forest.

You look up at this old tree, and is it absolutely so massive.

It also has a tiny door in its trunk.

It has strong branches that have dark green leaves that stretch out into the forest.

A gnome is sitting on a red-spotted mushroom by the doorway of the tree trunk.

The gnome now smiles at you and blows a magic puff of gold dust into the air.

The little door swings open very slowly.

You are now feeling very curious, and you step inside the old tree.

To your amazement, the tree trunk is hollow, warm, and very cozy.

There are soft, warm woven rugs placed on the floor.

There are pictures of stories, legends, and myths carved into the tree walls.

There are mythical and fairytale creatures all carved in and drawn into the wood of the tree.

You realize that anything is possible here.

This is the entrance to your enchanted and magical treehouse.

How would you like to get to the very top of your treehouse?

Well, to your surprise, you notice there are three choices for you to climb up inside the hollow old tree trunk.

You see a magical climbing rope that carries you straight upwards.

There is also a magical and enchanted staircase that goes round and round and creates a wind tunnel.

Or there is an enchanted and magical flying lily pad from the babbling brook.

This lilypad is big enough to stand on and will float you upwards.

Now I want you to make your choice.

Suddenly you are now up at the top of the treehouse!

Imagine this is the most magnificent treehouse you have ever been in and seen.

It is a massive treehouse with lots of rooms inside of it.

It also has different levels and stories for you to explore and play in.

How would you want to decorate each room in the treehouse?

You are allowed to paint them any color you wish.

There are rope ladders everywhere for you to climb upon.

There are also binoculars to look into and across the entire forest all around you.

There is also a telescope to look up and gaze at the planets and stars in space.

You give out a big sigh of happiness.

Wow, it is so wonderful here in this peaceful magical forest at your very own private treehouse.

What else would you like to have in your treehouse?

Just use your imagination now, and everything will appear right before you.

You can even invite your friends to come and visit you at your enchanted treehouse.

Which friends would you like to join you now?

Even animals are allowed to come and play with you here.

Which animals would you wish to cuddle and play with in your magical treehouse?

Whatever you wish to do and whatever you want to see is all possible now here in your magical enchanted treehouse.

Now you start climbing through the branches of the old tree.

You just found a bird's nest, some chipmunks and squirrels, and some butterflies that glow in the dark. You also find some other fantastic creatures in this old safe, and wise tree.

You feel so happy now and free.

Keep playing and climbing around.

This is your magnificent treehouse for as long as you wish.

When you hear my voice returns, it will be time to fall deeply asleep.

Have fun now in your treehouse, and I will be with you very soon.

After having so much in your treehouse, you know that now is the time for you to return home.

You wave goodbye to your fantastic forest friends.

What way do you want to travel back down the tree trunk?

Would you like to take the floating lilypad, the spiral staircase, or the magic rope?

Make your choice now.

You now have arrived quickly and safely down back to the floor of the tree.

The door mysteriously opens for you, and you step outside.

The old, kind, and loving gnome smiles at you and blows a magical golden cloud of dust over you again.

You are now starting to feel very very sleepy.

The moonlight shines down and sparkles the soft green grass path.

It is leading you back through the forest.

With every step you take, you feel more and more relaxed.

Sleepier and sleepier.

In your heart, your say thank you to the enchanted forest for this magical adventure.

The ancient forest starts to fade away, and you are now back in your warm and cozy bed.

You snuggle under the covers, and you fall deeply asleep.

You now have pure joy in your heart, and you can now dream fully happy.

This was the most beautiful treehouse in the entire world.

You now smile to yourself as you drift off into a comfortable sleep.

You know that this is your magnificent and magical treehouse waiting for you to return anytime you wish.
Sweet magical treehouse dreams.

(Music

25 Minutes

CHAPTER 3

Pirate Adventure

Now, as your eyes are closed, I hope you enjoy daring and exciting adventures because you are about to have the most amazing and fun journey you can imagine, full of surprises.
It is will beso brilliant it will feel like a dream.
As you close your eyes and listen, you settle into your coziest rest.
Your imagination can begin now to run free.
Explore all the beautiful possibilities of your magical dream coming true.
I wonder if you can believe that incredible legends are really possible.
Perhaps even legends that involve pirates, whales, and lost treasure.

As you just lie on your back, just let your arms and legs and even your belly relax.

You may feel yourself relaxing more and more as you take a deep breath in through your nose.

Let the airflow out.

Good.

Now take another few deep breaths in and out.

As you breathe, you may notice the air sounds just like the relaxing waves of the ocean flowing in and out so easily.

That's excellent.

You're doing great.

You are doing this bedtime meditation brilliantly.

As your eyelids completely relax, they are still gently closed.

Allow this sensation of the relaxing and calming ocean waves to really take over now.

Now start to imagine a big blue ocean wide and free with rolling waves that stretch out as far as the eye can see.

These waves are so relaxing to listen to.

As you really listen in, you think you may even hear the faint sound of a whale song far off in the distance.

All of a sudden, using your imagination, you visualize a pirate ship floating along the big blue happy waves.

As you start to see this ship, a picture is clearly forming in your mind's eye.

You are about to see how impressive this pirate ship really is.

You are now standing on the wooden deck of this incredible pirate ship.

As you look up and around you in amazement, you appreciate how huge it really is.

It is made up of timber like the big pirate ships in stories with an old, tall, and robust mast with large black sails.

At the helm of the boat, there is a brass statue that looks like a mermaid.

The most exciting thing you can hear and see is the flag that is flapping in the breeze.

This flag has a skull and crossbones painted on it.

This is the mighty flag of pirates.

You know that for sure, this is a pirate ship.

Suddenly lots of pirates emerge all around you on the deck of this ship.

You look around, and instead of fearsome and grim-looking pirates, they actually look so friendly and happy.

Instead of having scars on their faces, every one of them has a wide and welcoming grin.

They all look so genuinely happy to see you.

These are peaceful pirates who are welcoming you to their proud pirate ship.

You smile back at them, and you notice the peaceful pirates are all around the same age.

They explain to you that they have lots of fun sailing around the world and looking for long lost treasure.

Their mission is only to seek out treasures that are long forgotten buried in time where no one knows where it is.

The treasures that are buried deep beneath the depths of the deep deep ocean.

You listen to all this, and you immediately think this sounds so much fun.

You start thinking about exciting adventures you might take with them.

You wonder about it now and imagining a peaceful pirate hat on your head.

It is painted with the same symbol of their flag with a mermaid.

How amazing!

The peaceful pirates are officially inviting you to join them on their extraordinary adventures.

You are going on a voyage to find the glorious treasure chests that are said to be in a coral reef under the deep blue waves hidden by the most notorious pirate of them all.

Blackbeard.

Blackbeard was one of the most fearsome pirates who was said to have looted the most bountiful of pirate treasures in all the world.

One of the friendly pirates tells you in a whisper that only a very magical and special whale knows where the sunken mystery treasure is located.

The peaceful pirates have been searching forever for the treasure, but they have not found it yet.

Maybe you can help them find this very magical special whale.

Now you look up and see the beautiful horizon and the orange sun starting to set.

You feel so very satisfied to be here.

You are also starting to feel a little tired.

You just lie back into a hammock, swinging ever so gently on the deck just thinking about all of your happiest thoughts.

Thoughts of how you can help the peaceful pirates finally find this magical whale and Blackbeard's sunken treasure.

As you begin to sway back and forth, you are feeling so calm and relaxed even more.

Just relaxing to the sound of the ocean waves.

Just rocking back and forth in the breeze of the sea.

Just listening to the gentle sounds of the ocean relaxing you to sleep.

Deeper and deeper, you go to sleep.

The rhythm of the waves is lulling you to sleep into the magical land of your dreams.

Sinking Deeper and deeper down, down and further down into your most relaxing state.

You are enjoying this lovely safe, peaceful sinking feeling until you realize that the ship is actually starting to sink.

You jump up and look over the edge.

You see, the ship is now low in the ocean.

The water is about to spill over the edge into the ship.

Then all of a sudden, something incredible and surprising happens.

You are feeling the boat starting to rise up higher and higher.

You are now moving the opposite way, as if the whole pirate ship is being pushed up out of the water by a powerful, strong force pushing the entire ship back up again.

It is now resting easily on top of the safe, calm waves.

The peaceful pirates all let out a cheer as they quickly found and fixed the water leak by pumping all of the seawater out.

Now everyone is feeling relieved again, feeling entirely safe.

You are feeling a little curious as to what or who might have saved this mighty ship.

You and all of the peaceful pirates look together over the side of the boat, looking into the deep blue sea.

Suddenly there is a gush of water that sprays up into the air.

The water gushes so high, going higher than the mast of the ship.

Suddenly an enormous but very friendly face emerges above the breaking waves.

This is the most enormous face with the happiest and biggest smile you have ever seen.

You feel so much warmth and kindness in your heart as you recognize this lovely animal.

This is the biggest mammal on Earth.

He says, hi I'm willy the whale, but you probably know that I am a whale because of my blowhole and my size.

You laugh and nod at Willy the whale's voice.

Even all of your pirate friends laugh too.

You are feeling very brave now, and you step forward to thank Willy for rescuing all of you in the nick of time.

Willy says, no problem, I love helping friendly people out, and the peaceful pirates are always welcome in all of the seven seas.

You also ask Willy if he could possibly help you with something else.

You ask Willy if he knows the secret location of the hidden treasure.

Willy grins the biggest and widest grin showing his big white teeth.

Willy says, follow me to the treasure.
You humans are so funny thinking that things made out of colorful metal and stones are so important.
They are actually not that important to me, but it's okay I can help you locate the long-lost treasure chest with my sonar abilities.
They call me Willy the wise whale, and I can show you right now.
Come down and jump onto my back.
Just watch out for my blowhole.
Hold onto a barnacle or two.
You find it very easy to hang on safely.
You step carefully off the ship edge and jump off and onto Willy's huge smooth rubbery back.
It is actually really easy to just hold on tightly as you hang on to some of the bumpy barnacles, which are stuck to Willy's smooth rubbery skin.

You look behind you, and you see all the peaceful pirates wave and cheering for you.
Willy starts swimming, gliding, and takes off.
His strong whale fins cut through the frothy ocean waves.
Willy is the gentle giant of the sea.
He is even bigger up close.

You feel so free, loved, special and strong to have such an amazing and great friend at your side.

You see dolphins swimming alongside you, dipping and diving and squeaking with happiness and joy.
They are gliding along with you between the crashing waves.
Wow, these dolphins are so fun and so cheery and so happy.
They make you laugh so much with their squeaking.
Now something really incredible happens.
Willy is so wise and so kind.
He has such a magical and special type of energy.
Willy now gives you the gift of being able to breathe underwater.
Sit still and hold onto his back.
You both go down underneath the ocean through all of the bubbles.
You are gliding down together, getting deeper and deeper under the waves.
Right here, beneath the ocean, you look out around you and admire all of the ocean life around you.
It is such a spectacular sight to see.

You see schools of strange tropical fish all swimming around.

You see a magnificent octopus swimming by as well.

You even see some electric eels all living and swimming happily about.

What you love the most is the whale song of Willy.

He is singing loving, calming, and happy tunes.

You can now hear other whales singing along and back to Willy even though they sound very far away, but it is so clear for your ears.

It is so soothing and lovely to enjoy the music.

You realize the is the special sonar ability Willy has.

He is such an intelligent creature that is so pure of heart.

Willy is tracking the hidden location of the long-lost treasure for you.

Willy's song is so beautiful and becomes so charmingly pleasant and sings just for you.

Now when you dream of the ocean, it is full of surprises.

Just relax and sleep.

There will be treasure before your eyes.

Wow this is so amazing.

You can tell that Willy just loves to sing his beautiful, loving, and kind melody.

It makes you feel so safe and special and so much more relaxed to be here in this free open ocean.

Together you swim spiraling down and down into a marvelous and beautiful coral garden.

This coral reef garden has green seagrass with soft coral shining about with the most gorgeous colors.

You see so many types of fish.

Clownfishes, rainbowfishes and even angelfishes.

You swim down and down, and you see little tiny crabs of all different shapes, colors, and sizes.

You have now arrived at the legendary coral garden.

In the middle of the coral reef garden, resting in the center of these beautiful clams, is something that looks brown and shines with sparkles of metal.

It has seagrass growing on it and a peaceful seahorse resting on top of it.

As you get a little closer, you reach out and push the seagrass to the side.

Sitting in the middle of this circle of giant clams is what looks like to be the treasure chest.

It is wooden and has a brass gold lock keeping it shut firmly.

This must be Blackbeard's long-lost treasure chest. You have found it!

Willy swims closer to you to help you.

He opens his enormous whale mouth, and he clutches the chest between his big whale teeth and begins to swim you both upwards.

You are holding onto his back so excitingly.

You two are now gliding and swimming back up to the surface going higher and higher together.

You are moving smoothly up towards the pirate ship that is just waiting calmly in the distance that is swaying and rocking over the waves.

Willy sends up a magnificent and victorious spurt of sea ocean spray from his blowhole.

The peaceful pirates have spotted you through their telescope.

Everyone is so happy to see you and is now cheering for your return.

With the little lock between Willy's teeth, he quickly breaks the lock and spits the chest out with a flip of his whale tail.

You are all able to open the chest now.

You and the peaceful pirates open the big heavy chest lid together.

You open it, and it looks like sunlight is glowing out from the inside.

It is the most dazzling light that is being reflected from the glorious treasure.

The treasure has so many magnificent and brilliant ancient artifacts, gold coins, mini statues, chalices, precious gemstones, pearls, swords, and so many other treasures.

This is really a pirate's bounty.

You all have so much fun looking and feeling the treasure.

You all are leaping on the pirate ship and acting like real pirates.

You all are so happy, climbing up the mast and playing sword fighting.

You take the helm of the ship and have such amazing fun.

It feels so amazing and fantastic to be so free-spirited.

You are so happy to see all your new friends.

Willy stays for a while, laughing at all of you.

You all are being so silly with your treasure.

Willy also looks delighted too.

He gives you all a whale wave with his tail, gives a big spurt of seawater, and says goodbye.
You all wave and say thank you to the beautiful, gentle giant of the ocean.
With his huge mighty tail, he gives a big splash of water, and Willy disappears back beneath the waves of the ocean.
He continues to sing his lovely whale song.

Hmmm.
It is so soothing.
You start to feel so tired now.
So very tired as you climb back into the comfy hammock again.
You begin to rock along to the sounds of the ocean and the soothing whale songs of Willy the whale singing to you in the faraway distance.

As you rest here aboard the amazingly happy and loving pirate ship, you feel so much gratitude and love in your heart for Willy the whale.
He is such a kind hearted, generous and joyful creature to take you on your marvelous journey.

You two really have such an amazing time, and this is the greatest treasure of all.

As you begin to fall asleep now, you know that tomorrow you will wake up in your very own bed feeling so fresh and rested and so confident and happy inside.

So calm, confident, and happy to make your day tomorrow in the best possible way.

You are so courageous and brave.

You know that you can do anything in the world.

You are now drifting away, just sleeping and sleeping.

Floating and drifting into the most relaxing dreamland and just relax in that lovely land of pure magical dreams.

You are sleeping even deeper now.

Feeling so safe and so loved.

So blissfully wonderful to be the very special person that you are.

Sweat dreams.

42 minutes

CHAPTER 4

Wishing Waterfall

Now just lie down in your bed.
Make sure you get comfortable and listen along.
Just begin to relax more and more.
Let your sleepy and relaxing thoughts wonder about.
Now I would like for you to imagine visiting a very magical place.
An enchanted place where your every wish might soon come true.
If this sounds extra fun and extra relaxing to you, then you are in for a super special sleepy treat.
Very soon, all you need to do is to discover this very special magical wishing place.
Just close your eyes as you begin to use your wonderful imagination of yours just to relax more and more.

Let all of your daytime thoughts go as you begin to imagine and just dream.

It's becoming easier and easier to travel into your special dreamy place of wishes and really go there now.

Imagine a wonderful nighttime rainbow.

This rainbow takes you to a dream world full of possibilities that arrive as soon as you snuggle into sleep.

Just like a rainbow bridge that connects you to a far away distant land made up of many relaxing and beautiful colors.

The lovely rainbow pathway climbs all the way up into the sleepy nighttime sky above.

You can begin to imagine yourself on this wishing rainbow.

Now begin to imagine what your lovely rainbow bridge might look like.

You might even see your rainbow sparkle and glow with extra special wishing magic.

The fantastic rainbow bridge shines down on you.

It is so close beside you, shining down like a light beam all the way down through the stars of the night sky.

Maybe it shines down even through your own window.

It is almost as if you could reach out and feel these warm colors.

The light beams down on your hands and fingers.

You already know that this imaginary rainbow of yours is here to pick you up and float you along.

Very gently.

You are floating so happily.

Leading you all the way into the most enchanted and magical place at the end of this magical rainbow.

It is so soft and bouncy underneath your feet.

It is also very supportive.

It feels so safe and so strong.

Love imagining that you are walking, hopping, and bouncing on your rainbow.

You keep climbing up all the way into the sky.

Up and up you go until the rainbow bridge starts to bend back down again.

You are now moving down and down through the beautiful white fluffy clouds.

You are bending downwards on these light beams now.

You are going down and down even further until you see that there is a brand-new magical land full of magical wishes waiting here just for you.

You quickly realize that the rainbow has taken you all the way here.

All the way into the magical land of wishes that is suddenly below you.

You feel so excited now because your rainbow bridge has become like a curving slippery dip.

You sit down, and you slide, passing through the fluffy white clouds.

Suddenly you safely land, and you feel your feet touching the ground.

You feel yourself stepping down onto a soft green grassy hill landing so softly.

You find yourself stepping smoothly down and coming to a complete rest.

You are now sitting down happily underneath the shade of an enormous pink cherry blossom tree.

Now you look up and see this beautiful cherry blossom.

You must really be in the magical land of wishes.

Over behind the enormous cherry blossom, you can see a stunning enchanted waterfall flowing.

You know that this is the magical waterfall of wishes.

The waterfall of wishes has such clear and clean water.

It is almost as if it is a sparkling stream or a mist of shimmering magic in the air.

The water that falls here in the sparkling mist is the most gorgeous shade of blue that you have ever seen.

You now see even more magical colors streaming down as they all join with the clear blue water.

You now see shades of colors that you have never imagined before.

The magic of the waterfall glows brighter and brighter.

It shines even more marvelously the more you look at it.

You know that in your heart and in all of your thoughts, this impressive wishing magical waterfall has the power to bring your dream wishes to come right now to life.

Relax completely and rest.

Just be as calm and as happy as you wish to be, sitting peacefully under the pink cherry blossom tree.

You feel so happy and so relaxed.

It is as you haven't got a care in the world because the magical waterfall and your wishes are making it so.

Now you begin to wonder and imagine some of your most beautiful, most desired, and most favorite wishes coming true.

You gaze into this sparkly magical waterfall of wishes, and you decide to imagine just one of your happiest and kindest, most compassionate, most loving, and most exciting wishing coming true in real life now.

You know that this magical wishing waterfall only works for those wishes that are good, kind, loving, and the most helpful to everyone and especially if your wish makes you feel as happy as you can be.

The wishing waterfall will help you right now to this positive wish coming true.

Now, just imagine and start to make a wish.

Yes, just like that.

Go ahead and make your first special happy, loving wish.

As you do, what can you see?

What images or pictures does your happy wish look like?

Make it appear now in the magical mist of the wishing waterfall's beautiful colors.

Even as you wish it very quickly, you see the waterfall colors shine.

The magic mist of the waterfall sparkles.

You are seeing so many magical sparkles of the enchanting water bringing your happy, loving wish into real life now.

It is just like a movie.

You are watching more and more amazing details taking shape.

You see yourself joining with your wish.

You are now floating all the way into these happy, loving movie scenes.

You are now seeing yourself enjoying all the good scenes of your special wish.

You feel so good to also see yourself here in this magical happy movie.

You are now seeing yourself in all of these pictures and with all of these colors and even with all of the sounds and feelings, your special loving, happy wish.

It is brought into real life now.

You are seeing yourself feeling as happy as you wish yourself to be.

Now, as the waterfall glistens and shines, you keep feeling so very very happy.

Ask yourself if you have another special wish.

Imagine this wish coming true.

If you have another wish or even many have other wishes, you can wish for them now as long as these wishes are good and kind.

Just think of these wishes right now.

Very soon, you will see once again your magical wishing waterfall bringing every new wish clear into your life.

You see yourself joining into each happy scene feeling so good and being so very happy now as you just relax and continue to enjoy all of your special wishes coming true.

You are feeling so happy to continue exploring and to just keep making positive new wishes.

Imagine yourself moving into each of your amazing wishes.

Feel the loving and good wishes.

Always feeling better and better about yourself.

You are so much happier and positive to enjoy this incredibly special time in your life wishing your dreams.

Imagining yourself experiencing each wish coming into your life.

Now very soon, you are starting now to become so much sleepier.

You are feeling so very, very sleepy.

You know that it is time for you to sleep all the way into your bedtime dreams.

Take one last look at your waterfall of wishes feeling so happy to now be returning to your warm cozy bed.

You begin to see and feel the nighttime rainbow return.

All of the rainbow's light beams down to pick you up gently.

The rainbow bridge carries you all the way home.

All the way back down through your bedroom window.

You feel so happy and so calm all the way back into your warm and comfy bed.

As your body melts and relaxes, so do your thoughts. Relaxing soft into the soft mattress beneath you.

You feel your head resting on your pillow.

Your arms and legs feel so heavy now.

You are falling so happily and safely into your best sleep.

You are feeling so special and so loved as you drift deeper and deeper into your deep and happy dreams.

You will continue to dream with joyful delight.

You are dreaming about all of your most wonderful wishes coming true so very soon into your happiest life.

Sleep well now, and I wish you a sweet magical wishing waterfall dreams.

37 minutes

CHAPTER 5

Ancient Mountains

This sleep mediation is now going to take you on a fantastic and mysterious journey to meet a friendly dragon.

If you are ready to take the adventure to his hidden location high up the ancient mountains that are long forgotten, then close your eyes now.

Let your imagination run wild and free.

I want you to settle down into your bed.

I want you to get really comfortable.

Take a big deep breath in and a calm breath out.

You are doing amazing.

Take a deep breath in and a calm breath out.

Just breathe naturally and fully now.

You are feeling more and more relaxed.

You are doing great.

The meditation magic can only happy in the dreamy place of almost being awake and almost asleep.

Now imagine you are at a rocky mountain.
This mountain has a little bit of snow at the top.
These mountains are in a remote part of the world and are far away from where people live.
These are called the secret mountains that have not been explored yet by mankind for thousands of years.
Dragons are said that they no longer exist.
It is said that they have been driven to hide themselves at the most remote locations on Earth.
If you come by an abandoned cave far away from any human civilization, then it may just be the home of a dragon.

Imagine yourself walking along this mountain pass.
You have come here to search for the friendly dragon.
This narrow path along the mountains leads you up.
You know in your heart that you are very safe here.
It feels so fun to just explore the land.

The air feels so cool and refreshing, breezing across your face.

The landscape around you is so huge.

You can see the rocky mountains and rocky volleys as far as your eyes can see.

You have now made it pretty far up the mountain trail, and you start to see a massive castle built into the side of the mountain.

This castle looks abandoned, and vines are overgrowing on it.

Wow this place looks so fascinating and mysterious.

You notice a giant door where the entrance is located.

You feel so happy and excited.

Maybe this is where you will finally meet a friendly dragon.

You hope that this is where the friendly dragon lives.

You walk quietly up to the entrance of the cave and look inside.

A deep voice suddenly shouts out to you from within the castle.

It is like he already knew you were coming.

You shout back your name, and the deep voice calls out to you again.

Then suddenly, the cave starts to light up from deep within.

A golden light starts glowing all around you.

You can not see this dragon yet, but you step inside bravely and fearlessly.

You are so very confident and also curious.

You start walking through this massive cavern and twists and turns deeper and deeper into the mountainside.

There are wooden torches that start lighting up with fire all by themselves.

These start leading you through the darkness.

You still feel very safe here, and you know in your heart you will be protected.

As you follow and walk along, the cave opens up and gets bigger and bigger.

You immediately spot the dragon.

Such an immense, powerful creature with so many scales of so many colors.

He smiles and grins down on you.

Such a lovely big friendly grin.

He seems so very happy to finally see you.

You look at his scales, and they look so fascinating and interesting.

They all glimmer colorfully in the sparkling light.

His eyes are very shiny, and you can tell they are very kind.

As he moves towards you, you notice he has a tail.

He reaches out his claw to shake your hand.

You both laugh with happiness.

Wow you feel so lucky to meet a dragon in real life. This is one of the rarest and most mythical creatures in the world.

Take a moment and just chat with the dragon.

You now look around his hidden cave.

He has jewels and gemstones all around the cave.

You see so many gold coins and giant piles of treasure.

This friendly dragon tells you it is wonderful to be blessed with such nice things.

Although these things do not make him truly happy.

Yes, it is wonderful to have all these wonderful things, but he prefers gemstones and crystals because they have such positive energy.

He gets a little lonely all by himself.

He tells you that he has always been feared throughout history and fought in battles, but he has learned to still love his life deep down in his heart.

He is so much wiser after learning this wisdom.

He now uses his fiery breath for only love and kindness.

The friendly wise dragon smiles down on you with such a friendly grin.
He asks if you want to go flying with him.
He wants to show you this land of his.
You are so excited and say oh yes please!
You climb up onto his back, and you hold onto his scales.
He has a lot of fluffy fur on the top of his back.
The dragon starts to walk along through the cave now.
He is taking big and heavy steps.
You two reach the opening of the cave, and sunlight starts to appear.
He now suddenly jumps into the air and takes you flying.
The dragon's wings are now spread wide and flaps effortlessly through the air.
He is laughing so hard and booming now with so much happiness and love.
You two soar through the sky.
You are holding on very tight to the dragon.
You feel so safe, so protected, and very powerful on your strong, friendly dragon friend.
The wind is rushing through your hair now, and you are feeling so free.
You are now flying over the land below you.

The dragon points out places and where he has been.

You feel so very lucky and free to be living in a great time of peace.

It is such a great time to be alive on the planet right now.

You are so very lucky.

For your first stop, you two are going to explore the abandoned castle again near the mountain.

The dragon flies over the drawbridge onto the castle floor.

Wow, it is so fun to have this castle all to yourself.

You two walk inside and find a banquet room in the castle.

You find so many stairways and passages leading you out of the mountain top.

Wow this is so amazing.

You now hop back onto the back of your dragon friend.

Now you two explore the far reaches of Earth.

You two fly over tropical islands, see volcanoes, and even all the way up to the snowy tops of mountains.

You may now keep flying with your dragon flying over the planet.

You two explore everywhere with your new dragon friend.

Have as much fun in the world visiting some of the most amazing places.

When my voice returns, it will be time for you to have the most peaceful and happiest dreams.

After you have had the most wonderful and magical time with your dragon friend, it is now time for you to return home.

It is now nighttime, and the moon is shining high in the nighttime sky.

The dragon flies through the air.

He has such strong wings.

He is taking you all the way home.

You give him such a big hug.

You slide down his arm and into your bedroom window.

You wave goodbye to your dragon friend.

He gives you his big happy smile and then flaps his wings and flies off into the nighttime sky.

You now smile to yourself as you watch your dragon friend fly off into the night.

He is flying back to his cave in the mountains, to his home.

You now climb into bed and snuggle down under the warm blankets.

You breathe in a big deep sigh of gratitude and happiness.
This was such an amazing adventure.
Sleepiness is now taking over.
You are going to be lulled off into the most beautiful dreams.
You are going to dream and sleep so deeply now.
You feel so happy, so free, and safe.
You know that you are very powerful and confident.
You know that you can do anything.
You such an amazing and positive energy in your heart.
You are so wise, kind, and just like your dragon friend, you drift off into the most wonderful dreams.
You feel so blessed and loved.
You know that you can visit your dragon friend at anytime you want in his mountain side cave.
You can visit anytime you wish.
Sweet dragon dreams.

31 minutes

CHAPTER 6

African Safari Adventure

Welcome to the lion adventure journey for this part of the book.

This is a sleep meditation where you will be taken on a magical and mystical guided meditation adventure across the African savannah.

On this journey, you will meet extraordinary animals who will show the circle of life and for all that lives within.

If you are ready to have the most amazing journey with some fun, fascinating, and loving animals, then close your eyes and let your imagination run free.

Imagine you are now in a great big green African savannah plain.

This is where the animal kingdom roams free.

This is sacred land and is the home of the lions.

These lions only rule the land with strength and wisdom.

Imagine you are standing here in the African savannah.
You look around you, but you can't seem to spot any animals yet.
Just plain open grasslands.
Wow is it so relaxing.
Now take some deep breaths in and out fully.
In and out fully.
That's amazing.
You are doing wonderful.

You now easily imagine a fresh and gentle breeze of wind blowing across your face and into your hair.
The ground is soft and warm underneath your feet.
There is a lot of space all around you.
You see vast stretches of open land, making you feel so free.
You are filled with strength and courage.
You have so much curiosity, and you discover and suddenly see a huge tree in the distance.
You start walking towards it, and you feel something very warm next to you and brushes up onto you.
It is a lion!
This lion is not a fully grown lion yet but still bigger than a cub.
He has a little soft mane and such a friendly smile.
He looks so kind and silly, and you laugh along with him.

You both laugh, and he tells you he is headed in the same direction to the Tree of Life.

Wow, you feel so lucky to have such a great companion with you, and you feel so happy.

Walk and talk to your new friend.

He tells you his name, and you feel so happy and relaxed.

You two travel onward together towards the Tree of Life.

It is standing all by itself.

As you and your lion friend get closer, you now see that this is a very ancient and magical tree.

It has an extra thick tree trunk despite being on the warm and dry savannah grassland.

This tree has healthy, luscious, and green leaves.

It has such a great and wonderful energy about it.

There is a round patch ring of fresh green grass growing around the base of the tree.

You are admiring the grass and the tree as you walk around it.

You notice something quite extraordinary.

On the other side of the tree, sitting on the grass, is a baboon meditating.

You can't help but look and observe this baboon.

He has a red nose and blue cheeks.

He has a little patch of white hair on his head and looks old and very wise.

He is sitting cross-legged and is deep within his thoughts, just meditating.

He suddenly opens his eyes wide open, leaps up to you, and shakes your hand so vigorously.

He also pats your lion friend and welcomes you both with so much love, joy, and kindness.

He climbs up the tree, goes inside the hollow tree, and gestures you both to follow him inside.

You listen and follow him with excitement.

This is the baboon shaman, a mystical healer with so much wisdom, knowledge, and positive energy.

He knows the sacred knowledge about the planet.

You see, he has drawings of animals, lions, weather patterns, and ancient paintings explaining the circle of life all over his walls.

The paintings are explaining that this life energy flows and connects all living things and all living creatures.

Everything lives together in perfect respectful harmony generation after generation.

You immediately understand the balance of the ecosystem, and every single living thing and animal has a right to live peacefully in each of their habitats.

The baboon breaks open an orange fruit to share with the both of you.

You can ask the baboon anything you wish to know.

You can ask him anything you want.

Spend a couple of moments and chat with the old and wise baboon.

You feel so special and so honored to have visited this ancient tree and the shaman baboon.
He explains to you and your lion friend that he will make a great kind-hearted king one day.
You both wave goodbye to the wise baboon, and you both travel onwards to the jungle in the distance.

You now see a shallow river that flows along and trickles and winds through the African savannah and to the jungle ahead of you.
The water is so soothing and so crystal clear.
You both now enter under the shade of the cool jungle trees.
This tropical jungle has so many exotic plants and flowers.
You feel so very peaceful here and so welcomed.
The stream then turns into a tiny waterfall that crashes down into a blue pond.
Wow how beautifully refreshing this is.
You now see the most interesting animal just standing on a rock above the tiny pond.
You see its paws and chin are raised and moving his little head about.

It is a meerkat!
Wow, he is so funny and so cute.
You now start to hear branches breaking and footsteps stomping.
Suddenly a little warthog just jumps out and emerges from the jungle trees.
Then he jumps up, belly flops into the blue crystal clear pond, splashes water everywhere, and soaks the meerkat in water.
They both laugh, and you two go up to them to talk to them.
You and the lion become friends with the meerkat and warthog.
They are so funny, silly, and so jolly good to be around.
You all have so much fun together despite being such an odd group of individuals.
You all have fun adventures in the jungle, and they teach you everything they know.
Just relax, have fun, and just think positive.
You all then meet a female lioness who is so lovely and is friends with your lion friend.
Just have a few moments and just have fun with everyone here.

It is now nighttime, and your lion friend senses that it is now time to return home.
You all travel together back to the lion's home and across all of the lands in the savannah.

You all walk into the beautiful African sunset with your new friends.

Two lions, one warthog, a meerkat, and a very happy human all loving each other's company.

You now know that we can all live so happily and peacefully together in such harmony.

You now look ahead of you to the sunset.

You see in the distance, the wise old baboon is waiting for all of you.

You all have made it home.

Your lion friend has now fulfilled his destiny to become king.

This is the most sacred ceremony in the animal kingdom.

This ceremony uplifts your spirits and inspires you to do anything you want because you have a very special place in this circle of life.

Kindness, friendliness, wisdom, and love are all of the supreme sacred powers of positive energy that always prevails no matter what.

There is now a great massive celebration as all of the lions in the pride rejoice, having the new rightful king now returning home.

All of the animals in the kingdom arrive and circle around you all, and dance to the music.

All of the animals are celebrating together in such an amazing, fun, and peaceful way.

All delighted and feeling so blessed to have had such a fantastic meditation adventure with these beautiful animals.

It is now time for you to return to your warm and cozy bed.

This is where you will now dream deeply and sleep very peacefully now.

You will be in such bliss in your mind and heart.

You know that you are now a part of a very special place in the circle of life.

You belong with everything, and you are so very very loved.

You are now drifting off to have the happiest and most wonderful dreams.

You smile to yourself and know that you can visit your African savannah friends anytime you want for another amazing meditation adventure.

Sweet dreams.

20 minutes

CHAPTER 7

Magic Crystal Island

Now imagine a place where anything is possible.

This is a place where the most amazing things can happen to you right before your eyes.

This is the guided meditation for you to explore on your very own private and magical tropical island.

Close your eyes now and relax your entire body.

Remember that the meditation magic can only happen in that dreamy place of being almost awake and almost asleep.

Now imagine yourself standing on the shore of a beautiful tropical island.

You easily imagine the warm sand warming up your toes.

You look at the blue ocean in front of you.

The ocean is sparkling and glittering in the sunlight.

You watch the gentle and beautiful waves flow onto the sand and then out back into the ocean.
Take a deep breath in and a calm breath out.
Breath just like the flow of the waves of the ocean.
Each breath flowing in and out.
Just like the waves of the ocean.
Wow that is so wonderful.
You are doing amazing.

You now find yourself standing on your very own magical private tropical island.
It is so relaxing and peaceful here.
You feel so excited.
You know in your heart that there is so much for you to discover and explore here.
You start walking across the soft, warm sand beneath your feet.
A magical and gorgeous bird flies down to greet you.
It waves its wings to you and has the most colorful and pretty feathers you have ever seen.
What colors do you see on this bird's feathers?
The bird chirps proudly that he is the bird of paradise.
He will guide you around the island and show you everything there is to know.

This is your animal guide on this tropical island.
What is his name?
It can be any name that you wish to call him.
Your bird guide tells you that this tropical island is your special and safe place from now on.
You feel so very peaceful, and your heart is so full of joy.
You start walking through the palm trees, and you can see the magnificent sight before your eyes.
There is a beautiful and stunning waterfall.
The water splashes into a strong and gentle river glittering and shimmering in the sunlight.
The water looks so enchanting, and you watch as this waterfall is flowing so easily.
You feel so calm, and you suddenly notice that there are shiny rocks just hovering in the air.
It is flowing down little waterfalls.
Wow this is so amazing.
This is definitely an enchanting place to be in.
You can feel the healing energy of this place so easily here.
Everything is happening in perfect harmony now.
This your private tropical island of only pure peace, love, happiness, and magic.
As you look around the waterfall, you notice there are what looks like magical plants growing here.
The plants are so huge, tropical, and exotic.

They have such bright and amazing colors.
Wow it is so beautiful and marvelous.
Your bird guide tells you that there are also many animals living on your island.
Some of the animals you may have seen before, and some of them are magical creatures.
What animals do you want to see here on your tropical island?

Now your bird guide takes and leads you to the wishing cavern.
It is a very sacred and magical cave.
This is where anything is possible.
You walk through the wishing cavern and feel so very very special.
It is radiating and glittering with so much life energy.
It is glowing pink with sparkling rose quartz crystals.
There are so many crystals here radiating positive energy.
You are now standing in the middle of the cave and make a wish that is close to your heart.
You say your wish out loud now.
Your wish echoes through and around the cave.
All of the crystals start to light up with magical and positive energy.

Wow this is amazing.

Suddenly all of the crystals start growing bigger and bigger, rising up into the air.

Then a big piece of crystal flies over you like a hoverboard.

It seems like it wants you to step on it to go flying.

You step onto your magic crystal board, and you start flying out of the cave.

Your bird guide is flying along next to you, gliding through the air.

The wind is rushing through your face and hair now.

You are now flying over your tropical island.

You are soaring, dipping, and floating through the air, going faster and faster.

You look down at your beautiful island with such a stunning landscape.

Your bird guide is still flying right by your side.

You both laugh together with so much joy and happiness.

Wow this is so much fun.

You feel so light as a feather.

You feel so free.

You are flying on your magical crystal board.

You are exploring your very own magical tropical island.

Have some time to just fly and soar through the air.

Take some time to fly and float about.

Keep exploring and discover everything about this magical island.

When my voice returns, it will be time for you to have some deep and relaxing dreams.

You are feeling very sleepy now.

You have decided it is now time for you to return back home to your warm and cozy bed.

You and your magical crystal fly down through the air.

You hop off of your magical crystal board and onto the warm sand on the tropical island.

You now wave and say goodbye to your friendly bird guide.

The island now suddenly just starts to fade around you.

It is becoming cloudier and cloudier.

You can only see clouds of white around you.

Then the mist suddenly clears, and you find yourself back in your comfortable and safe room.

You are falling fast asleep now.

You feel so grateful for this incredible journey on your very own magical tropical island.

You now can start to just drift into your coziest and happiest dreams.

You are now falling fast asleep, going deeper and deeper.

You feel so special, so powerful, and so very loved.

You know that in your heart that this is your magical island.

It will always be here waiting just for you anytime you wish.

Sweet magical island dreams.

25 minutes

CHAPTER 8

Koala Grove

Hello and welcome to another relaxing and sleepy meditation.

This is an enchanting bedtime story that will take you on a fantastic journey.

Listen to my voice at it will guide you to the biggest island in the world.

Which is Australia.

Australia is home to some of the most amazing, exotic, cuddliest, fluffiest, and sleepiest animals on Earth.

Are you ready to meet all of the cutest animals in the world?

Amazing! I am too!

Now I want you just settle in and get very comfortable and cozy.

Close your eyes now and let your imagination run wild and free.

Think to yourself about how much you love animals.

Take a deep breath in and a long calm breath out.

Now just let your breathing continue to do this naturally all by itself.

Feel your body just relaxing.

Awesome, you are doing fantastic.

Now imagine you are in the Australian rainforest.

Imagine looking around and seeing big green trees and sunny blue skies.

Take in and breathe the beautiful fresh, crisp air.

You instantly feel at peace here.

You may have heard there is an old legend in Australia about a secret safe haven that is hidden deep within the land.

This haven is where the most cutest, cuddliest, and amazing koalas live.

This mystical place is called the Koala Grove.

This is a place where vast amounts of eucalyptus trees grow to protect the koalas from the outside world, even from forest rangers and nature lovers.

It is even hidden from bird watchers who have binoculars.

None of these people have been able to find this place because the exotic birds and clever kangaroos distract them on purpose to lead them off of the path.

The aborigine people were the first native people of Australia.

These people have lived here for thousands and thousands of years.

They know and understand the land's sacred energy, and they respect the circle of life here.

This safe Koala haven is so mystical and mysterious, and the Aborigines are the only ones who know the secret location.

The most skilled and expert Aboriginal trackers know that way to the haven.

You now breathe deeply in and use all of your senses now to help you discover your way to Koala Grove that is located in the heart of the Australian land.

You now spot a little honey-eating bird.

This bird is so tiny and just buzzes around with so much energy.

It has a yellow chest and hovers in front of you.

To your surprise, it can fly backward!

Only a few birds in the whole world can do this.

This bird zigzags back and forth.

Its tiny wings are just humming with so much vibrant energy.

You realize that this bird is trying to show you the way and to follow it.

You follow it for a while, and the honeyeater drinks nectar from the sweet flowers around you.

As you start to explore the land even more, you notice some very delicate purple wildflowers growing in a line.

It looks like it is a secret trail between the trees that are revealing the way to you.

You follow the purple flowers.

Then through the trees, you come to a water hole.

It looks so refreshing and relaxing.

You look at the crystal blue aqua water just gleaming in the sunlight like a turquoise gem.

Wow it is so beautiful.

This pond is covered with vibrant green lily pads with beautiful blooming flowers of white and pink all over it.

You look over the pond to see what's behind it.

It looks like it is shrouded in a white, soft mist making everything so hazy and cloudy.

It is tough to see, but you smell the eucalyptus trees stronger than ever before.

You realize that this could be a clue.

Koalas love to eat the leaves of eucalyptus trees.

You trust your senses, and you follow the wildflowers trail and the scent of eucalyptus trees and go into the mist.

You now arrive at the Koala haven.

It is a dense grove of the strongest, freshest and healthiest trees with the most amazing leaves and so many happy koalas.

These are probably the happiest koalas in the world.

An older grandpa koala crawls and waddles over to you.

He welcomes you to the Koala grove so kindly.

You look around you in awe and amazement.

You look at all of the adorable koalas around you, just relaxing with their families and just eating on the trees munching on the leaves, and just relaxing in the sunshine.

The grandpa koala tells you that these koalas love to sleep, but no other koala likes to more than me.

I sleep all day, and I am only awake for two hours to just eat some leaves and hang out with my family and friends here in the Koala Grove.

Here is the sleepiest and cuddliest tree.

You poke your head around the tree, and you see so many koalas just sleeping their day away.

They look so safe, so protected just being in their favorite spots.

This makes you feel so happy, and you just admire how cute and adorable all of these koalas are.

They all look so fluffy.

It makes your heart swell up with so much joy.

They all look like little cuddly fluffy teddy bears.

You just want to hold them all.

You notice that one of the koalas starts to blink his eyes and opens them.

He looks at you with such dreamy eyes making you feel so very sleepy.

You just want to doze off with them.

The koala smiles at you with his little mouth under his cute nose.

He waves his little paw at you, and you feed him leaves.

He starts to munch on them so lazily.

You gently reach out your hand and pat his soft fluffy furry head and feel his fluffy ears.

The koala reaches out to you and climbs onto your chest, wrapping around you with the coziest and warmest hug you have ever had.

You feel so blissfully happy and so peaceful.

You are hugging the cutest koala as he just nestles down sleepily on you like a big warm, soft teddy bear.

You feel so relaxed and starting to feel a little sleepy now.

With the koala dozing off, you are starting to feel dreamy as well.

You pet his soft, gentle fur and place him back to the spot on the tree where he was before.

You lie down on the grass below, and you take a nap.

You start to drift off into one of your happiest and most wonderful sleep safely in the comfort of the Koala Grove.

You are with your kind, sleepy, and loving koala friends.

You are feeling so very peaceful and proud that you trusted your instincts to lead you to this perfect place.

This place is so warm, calm, and cozy.

When my voice returns, you will have dozed off safely in the most blissful sleep like a koala.

I hope you have happy dreams, and may it be blissful and beautiful.

19 minutes

CHAPTER 9

Wolf Guardian

Welcome to this guided meditation to help you fall asleep.

This adventure is where your snow wolf will take you on a magical and mystical journey through the snowy mountains across the ice lands and winter forests.

If you are ready to meet your amazing and loyal guardian wolf, then close your eyes now and make sure you are ready to just relax and let your imagination run wild and free.

Now imagine yourself in a huge white snowfield that is surrounded by many trees.

Now imagine as you look around, you see there is no one else but you here just enjoying nature.

The air feels fresh, crisp, and cool.

You take a deep breath in and a long calm breath out.

One more time, take a deep breath in and a long calm breath out.

Feel your body relax as your breathing goes back to its natural rhythm.

That is amazing.

You are doing fantastic.

Perfect.

You are enjoying the open snowy nature space here in this big snowfield.

It is very peaceful here.

You now can easily imagine that it is around afternoon time and the sun is starting to set behind the snowy forest trees in the distance.

The sky is turning to twilight.

You walk through the snowy field, and you realize you have a long wool gray coat around your shoulders and snow boots on your feet to keep your feet and toes very warm.

Now you notice there are a small logs crackling and burning.

Perhaps this fire was started by people.

You still continue on in your journey but think hmm how mysterious.

The fire's embers are starting to die out as all of the wooden logs burn down in small orange flames.

You watch the smoke rise from the fire and twirls and curls in the air into the open snowy air.

Now you see through the smoke, and you see an outline of an animal.

This animal has bright eyes and watches you carefully and intently.

The beast steps forwards, and you see that it is your majestic and beautiful wolf guardian.

He looks so strong and healthy.

He has thick white fur to make sure he can withstand the cold and has a very kind and happy face.

This snow wolf is really big.

Wow he is so calm and brave.

You know that deep down, he is very wise and loyal.

This is a very special creature of mother nature.

You feel so lucky to be meeting your very own guardian wolf.

You reach out to touch his fur and say hello.

It circles around you and the fire without ever taking its eyes off of you.

Then it comes over next to you and bows its head.

You have so much happiness in your heart.

You pet this divine creature, and it has such soft white fur.

It now crouches down, and you sense that it wants you to climb onto its back.

You immediately climb on its back, and you can feel that he has magnificent strength.

You feel so very safe and so protected with your amazing new wolf friend.

You hold onto the wolf's lovely fluffy fur, and this wonderful creature takes you walking through the white snow.

It now starts to run gently, and you feel so much joy as your wolf breaks into a sprint.

It is streaking across the snow, running faster than you could ever think possible.

The cool crisp air rushes over your face and through your hair.

You feel so alive and so excited.

Your loyal wolf friend takes you to explore the icy wilderness.

Together you both run wild and free as you hold on tightly to the wolf's back.

It runs all across the snowfields and through the icy forest.

You notice that it has great instincts and intuition, and he fully trusts them and himself.

He navigates this icy wilderness with so much ease and wisdom.

You notice snow owls perched up in the trees, and they are all staring down at you with kind eyes.

Your wolf gives them a friendly nod as you both run by them.

You are now running past a completely frozen lake.

You notice and pass some huge polar bears looking for fish to eat.

They notice you, and they look so happy as they wave their paws to you.

Your wolf runs so quickly.

He is such a brave wolf.

After riding across the ice landscapes for quite some time, you stop by a mountain river with water trickling and rushing down made from the melted snow caps.

You cup your hands, and you drink the pure cold mountain water.

Wow it tastes so amazing, so fresh, and so clean.

It quenches your thirst and uplifts your mood and spirits.

Now your wolf friend starts drinking from the stream as well.

You feel so happy and lucky to have such a loyal companion with you.

You feel so spiritually connected to this amazing creature.

You know that this is an animal in your heart that you can tell all of your secrets to and truly trust with your biggest dreams, wishes, and deepest desires.

Your wolf guardian crouches down to you and nods for you to go on his back again for a final ride.

You are so curious and excited about where he is going to take you next.

You hold on tightly and give a pat on the wolf's back.

He now suddenly sprints up the mountainside and climbs up the mountain.

At the very top of this icy mountain, you see the most amazing and stunning view across the snowy countryside.

Wow it is absolutely breathtaking.
You see all the forests, lakes, waterfalls, and ice caps below.

At the top of this mountain, there is a gigantic tree.
It is the biggest tree you have ever seen.
You hop off your wolf guardian, and you walk up to look and admire the tree.
Suddenly you see wolf cubs playing about, just tumbling and chasing each other around in the snow.
You then notice there are also many other wolves just relaxing, resting, and gathered around this massive tree.
Your guardian wolf friend has taken you to meet his wolfpack.
They live at the very top of the mountain at the base of the giant tree.
You understand the wolf is showing how important loyalty and trust is, by bringing you to his home.
Now you suddenly feel such a deep bond with him, and you now know that you are always safe here whenever you need inspiration.
Trust your instincts, be brave, make wise choices, and remember you are always free and safe.

Some wolf cubs now run over to you, and you pet and play with them.
They are so cute and fluffy.
They make you laugh so much.

The moon has come out now, and it is a full moon.
The wolves all start to howl together in the moonlight.
You join them in a howl.
You feel so powerful and alive to really express your true self.
Your spirit soars with so much freedom and fun.
You feel so much gratitude and happiness for this amazing adventure.
You now know that it is time for you to return home.
You give your guardian wolf one last pet behind the ears and wave goodbye to everyone on the icy landscape.
Everything starts to fade around you, and you return to your warm and cozy bed.

You know in your heart that your loyal wolf guardian will always be there for you to visit anytime you wish.

Just smile and be happy to yourself, knowing this while you drift into your most wonderful and blissful dreams.

Sleep deeply now and feel so relax and wonderful.

You feel so brave, powerful, wise, kind, loved, and so inspired.

Now I wish you all of the happiest and sweetest dreams tonight.

17 minutes.

CHAPTER 10

Puppy Kingdom

Make yourself comfortable and close your eyes.
Take a big deep breath in through your nose.
And slowly and gently breathe out through your mouth.
Again big deep breath in and slowly and gently breathe out through your mouth.
One more time, big deep breath in and slowly and gently breathe out through your mouth.

Just relax and let your breathing come back to its natural rhythm.
Now I want you to imagine you are in a beautiful luscious green meadow field.

Flowers are growing all around the edges of this meadow field.

You can tell parts of this field have very young grass growing.

You can see the grass and plants blowing in the gentle breeze.

Here you are safe, loved, and well-protected always.

Take a look around you.

What else can you see?

Take a good look around.

You can hear rustling up ahead of you in the long green grass.

You wonder what it could be.

The grass is still moving about, so you set out to take a look.

You walk towards the moving grass, and what do you see?

You found a little black cute puppy.

It is all by itself on this big green field!

Well, it seems to be having such a great time just rolling about in the grass.

You watch the puppy just for a moment while it is having so much fun.

You watch it as it chases its own tail.

It is trying so hard to catch it.

You see a spot of white fur on one of its paws.

You decide to name the dog spot.

It suddenly stops because it sees you standing there just looking at it.

You don't want to frighten it anymore, so very gently, you reach out your hand for the little puppy to have a sniff so it won't be afraid of you.

The puppy seems to really like you!

It starts to jump up and down with so much excitement and starts licking you all over.

You gently pet and stroke the puppy's fur.

It feels so soft underneath your hand.

You now sit down and play with the little puppy.

You and the cute little puppy start to roll around in the grass, having such a fantastic time.

You are kind of worried that why is this little puppy all by itself.

Well maybe it is lost, but you hope it is not.

Then another dog just like him pops out of the long grass.

This dog looks just like the puppy but a lot bigger.

You realize that this dog is the puppy's mother.

She has been looking for her baby all over the place.

She runs up to the puppy and snuggles him so much.

Now the little puppy is so happy.

The puppy starts jumping all over its mother, and the mother looks at you with such loving and kind eyes.
Then all of a sudden, she talks to you.
You are absolutely shocked and flabbergasted.
This beautiful dog just spoke!
Oh my god!
You notice the mother has the same white spot as the little puppy.
They look so cute together.
She tells you that her name is Sweety.
Her puppy's name is Sam.
The little puppy is a boy, and she is so thankful to you for looking after her puppy.
She invites you to join them to a special place where other humans do not know about.
It is called the puppy kingdom.
She tells you to follow her, and you happily do.

You walk through the long and tall green grass.
You feel the bushes against your legs.
The little puppy sam is so happy and just rushes ahead of you.
He looks like he is having the time of his life, just smiling.

After a short while, you all come to a little white picket fence with a gate in the middle of it.

Sweety opens the gate, and you see on the other side is an absolutely amazing view.

It looks like a very large castle with so many details.

The whole castle is painted black with white spots all over it.

There is a pathway that leads to the castle.

You all follow it, and it takes you to the most amazingly large castle doors that you have ever seen.

They are gigantic and enormous.

The doors are also black with white spots on them.

It kind of looks like Sam and Sweety.

The big doors open up for you as if it was open by magic.

You step through to the other side, and you see what looks like a gigantic house of fun and play.

You can see so many bright and wonderful colors everywhere.

Wow it is so majestic and wonderful here.

In this castle, there are so many different sizes and breeds of dogs.

Big ones, small ones, thin ones, chubby ones.

There are so many dogs!

Pugs, beagles, golden retrievers, rottweilers, poodles, German shepherds, and so many more.

Sweety tells you that this is a castle that is solely run by dogs and puppies.

They even have their own king.

He has a very deep, commanding voice and is married to the queen.

This is a palace of pure fun and enjoyment.

Here is where you will be treated like royalty.

Oh how lovely.

Sweety tells you that you can take a good look around if you want to.

There are food, snacks, and drinks you can enjoy.

Wow you are feeling so lucky.

You now spot some small dogs all having fun and sliding down what looks like a big waterslide.

They all look like they are having so much fun.

You see a big swimming pool with some more dogs just swimming and playing about.

You see other dogs jumping off the diving boards and disappearing beneath the water.

Everyone looks like they are having so much fun.

You decide to enter the palace now yourself.

You really want to see what else is inside here.

Wow there are so many great things here.
The first thing that catches your eye is the racetrack.
It runs right through the palace and loops around back in the gardens.
There is a game room with everything you could possibly imagine here.
There is a trampoline, and you see dogs just flying so high above you doing some fantastic acrobatic tricks.
Wow it kind of looks scary and dangerous.
There is so much to do here.
Your head is spinning with so many options.
It is now your turn to go around the palace and do whatever you want.
Maybe you can play ball, swim in the pool, have fun on the waterslide, or jump on the trampoline.
Whatever you want to do, you can do it here.
Don't forget to eat the food and snacks.
So just for a little bit, decide where you want to go and what you would like to explore.
It is now time for you to have lots and lots of fun.

Did you have fun playing with all of your new puppy friends?

Did you see and experience all of the things you would like to?

Did you get yourself a snack and food?

You are feeling a bit sleepy now.

You wonder if you could just get some rest, and you notice Sam is sleepy as well.

He is even having a hard time keeping his eyes open.

Even Sweety is looking very tired as well.

Now all of you walk into another very large room.

This room is the biggest dog bed there has ever been.

It is the size of a small house.

Oh my it is so massive!

It is made up of the softest fur and has the biggest and softest cushions made up of feathers, and you know it was made just for you to lie down on.

Sweety gestures to the two of you that it is time for a little nap.

You both jump into a big soft dog bed and get really comfortable.

There are so many dogs here too.

You now just close your eyes and take a big deep breath in, and you slowly and gently breathe out.

You are so happy and so loved to be with Sam and his mom.

You are so happy you have met all of the other lovely puppies.
Your eyes are feeling very heavy now.
You really don't want to open them now, but that is totally okay.
You don't feel like you want to anyways.
Just lie here for a little while now.
A little snooze and nap never hurt anyone.
Just lie here and be safe.
You now know that you can always come back here to the puppy kingdom to see your new friends whenever you wish.
Just snuggle up next to Sam, and when you finally wake up, you will be in your very own bed.
You are feeling so refreshed, happy, and ready to start the new day when you wake up.

30 minutes

CHAPTER 11

Owl Spirit

Welcome to this special guided meditation where you will meet with your wise spirit animal.

Close your eyes now and take a big deep breath in and a long calm breath out.

That's amazing.

Feel your breath moving in and out like the waves of the ocean.

It is so simple and relaxing.

Just breath.

Feel your whole body starting to relax now as you prepare to meet your wise and powerful spirit animal.

Imagine a big green forest with giant ancient and wise trees.

This forest is shrouded in mist and knows everything about the history of the Earth.

Nature always remembers everything because energy is passed from one generation to the next.

These ancient and wise trees are home to an extraordinary and intelligent creature.

This creature is blessed with the wisdom to see everything and understand everything from the highest perspective.

It knows and will teach you how to be kind to yourself and kind to others.

It believes in the divine balance of the universe.

Imagine you are standing here in this misty forest.

You feel the soft green grass beneath your feet.

You can smell the damp Earth.

You can see the leaves and flowers of this ancient forest, and you feel a cool crisp, refreshing breeze blowing against your face.

You now spot a particular tree that has branches on the ground, twisting and turning.

The branches look like it is leading you up to the thick green leaves above.

You get a feeling that you should climb this tree.

Follow this inner voice in your heart, this feeling in your belly.

This is your intuition talking to you.

Listen to it.

You start to climb the tree with ease.

You feel so happy and so free-spirited.

You love climbing this tree and feeling the smooth and rough bark against your hands.

You find footholds to climb up and branches to cling on to.

You start to climb higher and higher.

You feel so special and so excited.

You are at one with this tree.

You are truly apart of nature now, and you feel like you belong here in the branches of this ancient tree.

Suddenly you have a strong feeling that you are being watched.

You look around you and see huge orange eyes looking at you from behind the leaves.

These eyes are so captivating and seems like it is hypnotizing you.

You could stare into these eyes all day.

You feel so curious and reach to push the leaves aside.

You see that these big orange eyes are from an owl.

You realize that this is a magical owl and one of the largest owls on the planet.

It looks so incredible and amazing.
It has such feathery wings and a lovely white coat.
It still looks at you with its golden orange eyes.
You know that the owl has excellent eyesight.
You sense that this owl can see beyond just sight.
He has the ability to see and feel everything with his mind.
It can sense instincts and intuitions.
You feel so connected to this owl.
This owl makes you feel like it is your best friend or even a family member.
You are so calm, so peaceful, so safe, and so loved here in the branches with your new owl friend.

You realize that this owl is your spirit animal.
It will guide you and protect you.
It will also help you discover your own wisdom and power.
Does your spirit animal have a name?
The wisdom of the owl connects with you.
You may ask it anything you want.
You may ask it for some advice.
Or you may even want to ask whatever it is you wish to know.
Feel your thoughts and answers clarify in your mind.

After talking to your spirit animal for a bit with your mind, it asks if you would want to go for a fly over the forest.

Wow how exciting this would be!

You are so honored and say yes with so much joy in your heart.

The owl blinks his eyes three times, and suddenly golden enchanted sparkles light up around the owl.

It is now growing bigger and bigger and now big enough for you to climb onto its back!

Hold on tightly to some of his fluffy feathers.

Wow he feels so soft and smooth.

You now both go up, flying higher and higher up and away.

You both are flying so freely now high up over the ancient treetops.

You feel so free and powerful.

It feels like you can do anything.

From here in the sky, you can see the sun setting on the horizon.

Wow such a magical view with just a little bit of warm orange daylight left.

Is there a special place you would like your spirit guide to take you?

Wherever you wish to go or whatever you wish to see.

Think about it in your heart now, and your owl will fly you there.

Is there anything else you would to ask your owl?
As you fly together soaring through the sky, you are able to ask it anything you wish.
You both fly over a lake that is glowing blue between the trees.
Together you both glide and soar over a waterfall, and it is flowing so peacefully down and into a little river.
You both now fly over the mystical and ancient mountains.
Wow these are so beautiful and magnificent, with everything covered in dark green.

It is now nighttime now, and you notice the moon is high up in the sky.
The stars have come out to shine and play, sparkling and lighting up the darkness around you.
The starlight is twinkling down over the ancient forest.
The owl now flies you home.

Together, you are still soaring through the sky and back to your room, where you are now relaxing so peacefully and happy.

You pet the soft feather and beautiful coat of this extraordinary animal spirit guide before it flies off.

You say a big thank you in your mind because you know that your spirit animal is always watching out for you.

It will always be there to guide you with all the wisdom, kindness, love, and strength.

Your spirit animal is always ready to share its universal wisdom with you.

You feel so relaxed and sleepy now.

You feel so safe, so peaceful, and filled with so much happiness in your heart.

Sweet dreams.

20 minutes

CHAPTER 12

Limiting Belief Buster

Many of the limiting beliefs we have stem from our childhood.

Children are young and can be shaped and molded by their surroundings with relative ease.

If we can successfully program our subconscious mind with ideas of success, confidence, and self love, then there is no limit to what we can achieve in life.

Here in this last part of the audiobook is a list of affirmations that should be played on repeat and even can be recited as repetitions is sure way to program our subconscious mind.

Play this for you and your child all night on a low comfortable volume, and you can even repeat it throughout the entire day.

Use these affirmations for 31 days or longer for the best results.

I am wise, brilliant and wonderful.
I love myself deeply.
I believe in my ability to succeed.
I am smart.
I am brilliant.
I am intelligent.
I am a fast learner.
Learning is fun and exciting.
I read, write and learn very quickly.
I have many gifts and talents.
I make wise decisions.
I enjoy eating healthy foods.
I am destined to live a life of prosperity.
My thoughts create my world.
All is well in my world.
I think positive thus creating a positive world.
My positive attitude attracts positive situations and positive circumstances.
What I think about often eventually becomes my reality.
I attract situations that matches how I feel.
I visualize what I want often.
I talk about what I want often.
I think about what I want often.
I am a kind and generous person.

I show compassion towards others.
I treat people how I want to be treated.
What I do to others I actually do to myself.
I take my schoolwork very seriously.
I am dedicated to being a wonderful student.
There isn't anything that I cannot be, do or have.
I excel in my academics.
I am a natural born leader.
I am strong fit and athletic.
My mind is powerful and I use it wisely.
I am safe.
I am loved.
I am friendly.
I am brave.
I am courageous.
I am a winner.
I am very creative.
I believe in myself.
I trust my abilities.
I am confident.
I make friends easily.
I am a good person.
I am a good friend.
I always overcome my challenges.
I believe in my abilities.
I listen to my inner wisdom.
I am tough and durable.

I can do anything.
I am completely unlimited.
I only think about the things I want to happen.
I am honest.
I am forgiving.
I am trustworthy.
I am very responsible.
I take care of my responsibilities.
I am wealthy.
I am prosperous.
I am abundant.
I am divinely protected.
I think big.
I believe in myself and my abilities.
I am extremely confident.
I have the courage to by myself.
I love me.
I am a bright student.
I value my education.
Obtaining knowledge is very important to me.
I love and value my family.
I go after what I want and I accomplish my goals.
I am a go getter.
My thoughts are very powerful and I choose them carefully.
I am brilliant wise and wonderful.
I love myself deeply.

I believe in my ability to succeed.
I am smart.
I am brilliant.
I am intelligent.
I am a fast learner.
Learning is fun and exciting.
I read write and learn very quickly.
I have many gifts and talents.
I make wise decisions.
I enjoy eating healthy foods.
I am destined to live a life of prosperity.
My thoughts create my world.
All is well in my world.
I think positive thus creating a positive world.
My positive attitude attracts positive situations and positive circumstances.
What I think about often eventually becomes my reality.
I attract situations that matches how I feel.
I visualize what I want often.
I talk about what I want often.
I think about what I want often.
I am a kind and generous person.
I show compassion towards others.
I treat people how I want to be treated.
What I do to others I actually do to myself.
I take my schoolwork very seriously.

I am dedicated to being a wonderful student.
There isn't anything that I cannot be do or have.
I excel in my academics.
I am a natural born leader.
I am strong fit and athletic.
My mind is powerful.
I use it wisely.
I am safe.
I am loved.
I am friendly.
I am brave.
I am courageous.
I am a winner.
I am very creative.

I believe in myself.
I trust in my abilities.
I am confident.
I make friends easily.
I am a good person.
I am a good friend.
I always overcome my challenges.
I believe in my abilities.
I listen to my inner wisdom.
I am tough and durable.

I can do anything.
I am completely unlimited.
I only think about things I want to happen.
I am honest.
I am forgiving.
I am trustworthy.
I am very responsible.
I take care of my responsibilities.
I am wealthy.
I am prosperous.
I am abundant.
I am divinely protected.
I think big.
I believe in myself and my abilities.
I am extremely confident.
I have the courage to by myself.
I love me.
I am a bright student.
I value my education.
Obtaining knowledge is very important to me.
I love and value my family.
I go after what I want and I accomplish my goals.
I am a go getter.
My thoughts are very powerful and I choose them carefully.
I am brilliant wise and wonderful.
I love myself deeply.

I believe in my ability to succeed.
I am smart.
I am brilliant.
I am intelligent.
I am a fast learner.
Learning is fun and exciting.
I read, write and learn very quickly.
I have many gifts and talents.
I make wise decisions.
I enjoy eating healthy foods.
I am destined to live a life of prosperity.
My thoughts create my world.
All is well in my world.
I think positive thus creating a positive world.
My positive attitude attracts positive situations and positive circumstances.
What I think about often eventually becomes my reality.
I attract situations that matches how I feel.
I visualize what I want often.
I talk about what I want often.
I think about what I want often.
I am a kind and generous person.
I show compassion towards others.
I treat people how I want to be treated.
What I do to others I actually do myself.
I take my schoolwork very seriously.

I am dedicated to being a wonderful student.
There isn't anything that I cannot be do or have.
I excel in my academics.
I am a natural born leader.
I am strong fit and athletic.
My mind is powerful and I use it wisely.
I am safe.
I am loved.
I am friendly.
I am brave.
I am courageous.
I am a winner.
I am very creative.
I believe in myself.
I trust my abilities.
I am confident.
I make friends easily.
I am a good person.
I am a good friend.
I always overcome my challenges.
I believe in my abilities.
I listen to my inner wisdom.
I am tough and durable.
I can do anything.
I am completely unlimited.
I only think about the things I want to happen.
I am honest.

I am forgiving.
I am trustworthy.
I am very responsible.
I take care of my responsibilities.
I am wealthy.
I am prosperous.
I am abundant.
I am divinely protected.
I think big.
I believe in myself and my abilities.
I am extremely confident.

I have the courage to by myself.
I love me.
I am a bright student.
I value my education.
Obtaining knowledge is very important to me.
I love and value my family.
I go after what I want and I accomplish my goals.
I am a go getter.

My thoughts are very powerful and I choose them carefully.

I am brilliant wise and wonderful.
I love myself deeply.
I believe in my ability to succeed.
I am smart.
I am brilliant.
I am intelligent.
I am a fast learner.
Learning is fun and exciting.
I read, write and learn very quickly.
I have many gifts and talents.
I make wise decisions.
I enjoy eating healthy foods.
I am destined to live a life of prosperity.
My thoughts create my world.
All is well in my world.
I think positive thus creating a positive world.
My positive attitude attracts positive situations and positive circumstances.
What I think about often eventually becomes my reality.
I attract situations that matches how I feel.
I visualize what I want often.
I talk about what I want often.
I think about what I want often.
I am a kind and generous person.
I show compassion towards others.
I treat people how I want to be treated.

What I do to others I actually do to myself.
I take my schoolwork very seriously.
I am dedicated to being a wonderful student.
There isn't anything that I cannot be do or have.
I excel in my academics.
I am a natural born leader.
I am strong fit and athletic.
My mind is powerful.
I use it wisely.
I am safe.
I am loved.
I am friendly.
I am brave.
I am courageous.
I am a winner.
I am very creative.

I believe in myself.
I trust in my abilities.
I am confident.
I make friends easily.
I am a good person.
I am a good friend.
I always overcome my challenges.
I believe in my abilities.

I listen to my inner wisdom.
I am tough and durable.
I can do anything.
I am completely unlimited.
I only think about things I want to happen.
I am honest.
I am forgiving.
I am trustworthy.
I am very responsible.
I take care of my responsibilities.
I am wealthy.
I am prosperous.
I am abundant.
I am divinely protected.
I think big.
I believe in myself and my abilities.
I am extremely confident.
I have the courage to by myself.
I love me.
I am a bright student.
I value my education.
Obtaining knowledge is very important to me.
I love and value my family.
I go after what I want and I accomplish my goals.
I am a go getter.
My thoughts are very powerful and I choose them carefully.

I am brilliant wise and wonderful.
I love myself deeply.
I believe in my ability to succeed.
I am smart.
I am brilliant.
I am intelligent.
I am a fast learner.
Learning is fun and exciting.
I read write and learn very quickly.
I have many gifts and talents.
I make wise decisions.
I enjoy eating healthy foods.
I am destined to live a life of prosperity.
My thoughts create my world.
All is well in my world.
I think positive thus creating a positive world.
My positive attitude attracts positive situations and positive circumstances.
What I think about often eventually becomes my reality.
I attract situations that matches how I feel.
I visualize what I want often.
I talk about what I want often.
I think about what I want often.
I am a kind and generous person.
I show compassion towards others.
I treat people how I want to be treated.

What I do to others I actually do myself.
I take my schoolwork very seriously.
I am dedicated to being a wonderful student.
There isn't anything that I cannot be do or have.
I excel in my academics.
I am a natural born leader.
I am strong fit and athletic.
My mind is powerful and I use it wisely.
I am safe.
I am loved.
I am friendly.
I am brave.
I am courageous.
I am a winner.
I am very creative.
I believe in myself.
I trust my abilities.
I am confident.
I make friends easily.
I am a good person.
I am a good friend.
I always overcome my challenges.
I believe in my abilities.
I listen to my inner wisdom.
I am tough and durable.
I can do anything.
I am completely unlimited.

I only think about the things I want to happen.
I am honest.
I am forgiving.
I am trustworthy.
I am very responsible.
I take care of my responsibilities.
I am wealthy.
I am prosperous.
I am abundant.
I am divinely protected.
I think big.
I believe in myself and my abilities.
I am extremely confident.

I have the courage to by myself.
I love me.
I am a bright student.
I value my education.
Obtaining knowledge is very important to me.
I love and value my family.
I go after what I want and I accomplish my goals.
I am a go getter.

My thoughts are very powerful and I choose them carefully.
I am brilliant wise and wonderful.
I love myself deeply.
I believe in my ability to succeed.
I am smart.
I am brilliant.
I am intelligent.
I am a fast learner.
Learning is fun and exciting.
I read write and learn very quickly.
I have many gifts and talents.
I make wise decisions.
I enjoy eating healthy foods.
I am destined to live a life of prosperity.
My thoughts create my world.
All is well in my world.
I think positive thus creating a positive world.
My positive attitude attracts positive situations and positive circumstances.
What I think about often eventually becomes my reality.
I attract situations that matches how I feel.
I visualize what I want often.
I talk about what I want often.
I think about what I want often.
I am a kind and generous person.

I show compassion towards others.
I treat people how I want to be treated.
What I do to others I actually do to myself.
I take my schoolwork very seriously.
I am dedicated to being a wonderful student.
There isn't anything that I cannot be do or have.
I excel in my academics.
I am a natural born leader.
I am strong fit and athletic.
My mind is powerful.
I use it wisely.
I am safe.
I am loved.
I am friendly.
I am brave.
I am courageous.
I am a winner.
I am very creative.

I believe in myself.
I trust in my abilities.
I am confident.
I make friends easily.
I am a good person.
I am a good friend.

I always overcome my challenges.
I believe in my abilities.
I listen to my inner wisdom.
I am tough and durable.
I can do anything.
I am completely unlimited.
I only think about things I want to happen.
I am honest.
I am forgiving.
I am trustworthy.
I am very responsible.
I take care of my responsibilities.
I am wealthy.
I am prosperous.
I am abundant.
I am divinely protected.
I think big.
I believe in myself and my abilities.
I am extremely confident.
I have the courage to by myself.
I love me.
I am a bright student.
I value my education.
Obtaining knowledge is very important to me.
I love and value my family.
I go after what I want and I accomplish my goals.
I am a go getter.

My thoughts are very powerful and I choose them carefully.
I am brilliant wise and wonderful.
I love myself deeply.
I believe in my ability to succeed.
I am smart.
I am brilliant.
I am intelligent.
I am a fast learner.
Learning is fun and exciting.
I read write and learn very quickly.
I have many gifts and talents.
I make wise decisions.
I enjoy eating healthy foods.
I am destined to live a life of prosperity.
My thoughts create my world.
All is well in my world.
I think positive thus creating a positive world.
My positive attitude attracts positive situations and positive circumstances.
What I think about often eventually becomes my reality.
I attract situations that matches how I feel.
I visualize what I want often.
I talk about what I want often.
I think about what I want often.
I am a kind and generous person.

I show compassion towards others.
I treat people how I want to be treated.
What I do to others I actually do myself.
I take my schoolwork very seriously.
I am dedicated to being a wonderful student.
There isn't anything that I cannot be do or have.
I excel in my academics.
I am a natural born leader.
I am strong fit and athletic.
My mind is powerful and I use it wisely.
I am safe.
I am loved.
I am friendly.
I am brave.
I am courageous.
I am a winner.
I am very creative.
I believe in myself.
I trust my abilities.
I am confident.
I make friends easily.
I am a good person.
I am a good friend.
I always overcome my challenges.
I believe in my abilities.
I listen to my inner wisdom.
I am tough and durable.

I can do anything.
I am completely unlimited.
I only think about the things I want to happen.
I am honest.
I am forgiving.
I am trustworthy.
I am very responsible.
I take care of my responsibilities.
I am wealthy.
I am prosperous.
I am abundant.
I am divinely protected.
I think big.
I believe in myself and my abilities.
I am extremely confident.

I have the courage to by myself.
I love me.
I am a bright student.
I value my education.
Obtaining knowledge is very important to me.
I love and value my family.
I go after what I want and I accomplish my goals.
I am a go getter.

My thoughts are very powerful and I choose them carefully.
I am brilliant wise and wonderful.
I love myself deeply.
I believe in my ability to succeed.
I am smart.
I am brilliant.
I am intelligent.
I am a fast learner.
Learning is fun and exciting.
I read write and learn very quickly.
I have many gifts and talents.
I make wise decisions.
I enjoy eating healthy foods.
I am destined to live a life of prosperity.
My thoughts create my world.
All is well in my world.
I think positive thus creating a positive world.
My positive attitude attracts positive situations and positive circumstances.
What I think about often eventually becomes my reality.
I attract situations that matches how I feel.
I visualize what I want often.
I talk about what I want often.
I think about what I want often.
I am a kind and generous person.

I show compassion towards others.
I treat people how I want to be treated.
What I do to others I actually do to myself.
I take my schoolwork very seriously.
I am dedicated to being a wonderful student.
There isn't anything that I cannot be do or have.
I excel in my academics.
I am a natural born leader.
I am strong fit and athletic.
My mind is powerful.
I use it wisely.
I am safe.
I am loved.
I am friendly.
I am brave.
I am courageous.
I am a winner.
I am very creative.

I believe in myself.
I trust in my abilities.
I am confident.
I make friends easily.
I am a good person.
I am a good friend.

I always overcome my challenges.
I believe in my abilities.
I listen to my inner wisdom.
I am tough and durable.
I can do anything.
I am completely unlimited.
I only think about things I want to happen.
I am honest.
I am forgiving.
I am trustworthy.
I am very responsible.
I take care of my responsibilities.
I am wealthy.
I am prosperous.
I am abundant.
I am divinely protected.
I think big.
I believe in myself and my abilities.
I am extremely confident.
I have the courage to by myself.
I love me.
I am a bright student.
I value my education.
Obtaining knowledge is very important to me.
I love and value my family.
I go after what I want and I accomplish my goals.
I am a go getter.

My thoughts are very powerful and I choose them carefully.
I am brilliant wise and wonderful.
I love myself deeply.
I believe in my ability to succeed.
I am smart.
I am brilliant.
I am intelligent.
I am a fast learner.
Learning is fun and exciting.
I read write and learn very quickly.
I have many gifts and talents.
I make wise decisions.
I enjoy eating healthy foods.
I am destined to live a life of prosperity.
My thoughts create my world.
All is well in my world.
I think positive thus creating a positive world.
My positive attitude attracts positive situations and positive circumstances.
What I think about often eventually becomes my reality.
I attract situations that matches how I feel.
I visualize what I want often.
I talk about what I want often.
I think about what I want often.
I am a kind and generous person.

I show compassion towards others.
I treat people how I want to be treated.
What I do to others I actually do myself.
I take my schoolwork very seriously.
I am dedicated to being a wonderful student.
There isn't anything that I cannot be do or have.
I excel in my academics.
I am a natural born leader.
I am strong fit and athletic.
My mind is powerful and I use it wisely.
I am safe.
I am loved.
I am friendly.
I am brave.
I am courageous.
I am a winner.
I am very creative.
I believe in myself.
I trust my abilities.
I am confident.
I make friends easily.
I am a good person.
I am a good friend.
I always overcome my challenges.
I believe in my abilities.
I listen to my inner wisdom.
I am tough and durable.

I can do anything.
I am completely unlimited.
I only think about the things I want to happen.
I am honest.
I am forgiving.
I am trustworthy.
I am very responsible.
I take care of my responsibilities.
I am wealthy.
I am prosperous.
I am abundant.
I am divinely protected.
I think big.
I believe in myself and my abilities.
I am extremely confident.

I have the courage to by myself.
I love me.
I am a bright student.
I value my education.
Obtaining knowledge is very important to me.
I love and value my family.
I go after what I want and I accomplish my goals.
I am a go getter.

My thoughts are very powerful and I choose them carefully.
I am brilliant wise and wonderful.
I love myself deeply.
I believe in my ability to succeed.
I am smart.
I am brilliant.
I am intelligent.
I am a fast learner.
Learning is fun and exciting.
I read write and learn very quickly.
I have many gifts and talents.
I make wise decisions.
I enjoy eating healthy foods.
I am destined to live a life of prosperity.
My thoughts create my world.
All is well in my world.
I think positive thus creating a positive world.
My positive attitude attracts positive situations and positive circumstances.
What I think about often eventually becomes my reality.
I attract situations that matches how I feel.
I visualize what I want often.
I talk about what I want often.
I think about what I want often.
I am a kind and generous person.

I show compassion towards others.
I treat people how I want to be treated.
What I do to others I actually do to myself.
I take my schoolwork very seriously.
I am dedicated to being a wonderful student.
There isn't anything that I cannot be do or have.
I excel in my academics.
I am a natural born leader.
I am strong fit and athletic.
My mind is powerful.
I use it wisely.
I am safe.
I am loved.
I am friendly.
I am brave.
I am courageous.
I am a winner.
I am very creative.

I believe in myself.
I trust in my abilities.
I am confident.
I make friends easily.
I am a good person.
I am a good friend.

I always overcome my challenges.
I believe in my abilities.
I listen to my inner wisdom.
I am tough and durable.
I can do anything.
I am completely unlimited.
I only think about things I want to happen.
I am honest.
I am forgiving.
I am trustworthy.
I am very responsible.
I take care of my responsibilities.
I am wealthy.
I am prosperous.
I am abundant.
I am divinely protected.
I think big.
I believe in myself and my abilities.
I am extremely confident.
I have the courage to by myself.
I love me.
I am a bright student.
I value my education.
Obtaining knowledge is very important to me.
I love and value my family.
I go after what I want and I accomplish my goals.
I am a go getter.

My thoughts are very powerful and I choose them carefully.
I am brilliant wise and wonderful.
I love myself deeply.
I believe in my ability to succeed.
I am smart.
I am brilliant.
I am intelligent.
I am a fast learner.
Learning is fun and exciting.
I read write and learn very quickly.
I have many gifts and talents.
I make wise decisions.
I enjoy eating healthy foods.
I am destined to live a life of prosperity.
My thoughts create my world.
All is well in my world.
I think positive thus creating a positive world.
My positive attitude attracts positive situations and positive circumstances.
What I think about often eventually becomes my reality.
I attract situations that matches how I feel.
I visualize what I want often.
I talk about what I want often.
I think about what I want often.
I am a kind and generous person.

I show compassion towards others.
I treat people how I want to be treated.
What I do to others I actually do myself.
I take my schoolwork very seriously.
I am dedicated to being a wonderful student.
There isn't anything that I cannot be do or have.
I excel in my academics.
I am a natural born leader.
I am strong fit and athletic.
My mind is powerful and I use it wisely.
I am safe.
I am loved.
I am friendly.
I am brave.
I am courageous.
I am a winner.
I am very creative.
I believe in myself.
I trust my abilities.
I am confident.
I make friends easily.
I am a good person.
I am a good friend.
I always overcome my challenges.
I believe in my abilities.
I listen to my inner wisdom.
I am tough and durable.

I can do anything.
I am completely unlimited.
I only think about the things I want to happen.
I am honest.
I am forgiving.
I am trustworthy.
I am very responsible.
I take care of my responsibilities.
I am wealthy.
I am prosperous.
I am abundant.
I am divinely protected.
I think big.
I believe in myself and my abilities.
I am extremely confident.

I have the courage to by myself.
I love me.
I am a bright student.
I value my education.
Obtaining knowledge is very important to me.
I love and value my family.
I go after what I want and I accomplish my goals.
I am a go getter.

My thoughts are very powerful and I choose them carefully.
I am brilliant wise and wonderful.
I love myself deeply.
I believe in my ability to succeed.
I am smart.
I am brilliant.
I am intelligent.
I am a fast learner.
Learning is fun and exciting.
I read write and learn very quickly.
I have many gifts and talents.
I make wise decisions.
I enjoy eating healthy foods.
I am destined to live a life of prosperity.
My thoughts create my world.
All is well in my world.
I think positive thus creating a positive world.
My positive attitude attracts positive situations and positive circumstances.
What I think about often eventually becomes my reality.
I attract situations that matches how I feel.
I visualize what I want often.
I talk about what I want often.
I think about what I want often.
I am a kind and generous person.

I show compassion towards others.
I treat people how I want to be treated.
What I do to others I actually do to myself.
I take my schoolwork very seriously.
I am dedicated to being a wonderful student.
There isn't anything that I cannot be do or have.
I excel in my academics.
I am a natural born leader.
I am strong fit and athletic.
My mind is powerful.
I use it wisely.
I am safe.
I am loved.
I am friendly.
I am brave.
I am courageous.
I am a winner.
I am very creative.

I believe in myself.
I trust in my abilities.
I am confident.
I make friends easily.
I am a good person.
I am a good friend.

I always overcome my challenges.
I believe in my abilities.
I listen to my inner wisdom.
I am tough and durable.
I can do anything.
I am completely unlimited.
I only think about things I want to happen.
I am honest.
I am forgiving.
I am trustworthy.
I am very responsible.
I take care of my responsibilities.
I am wealthy.
I am prosperous.
I am abundant.
I am divinely protected.
I think big.
I believe in myself and my abilities.
I am extremely confident.
I have the courage to by myself.
I love me.
I am a bright student.
I value my education.
Obtaining knowledge is very important to me.
I love and value my family.
I go after what I want and I accomplish my goals.
I am a go getter.

My thoughts are very powerful and I choose them carefully.
I am brilliant wise and wonderful.
I love myself deeply.
I believe in my ability to succeed.
I am smart.
I am brilliant.
I am intelligent.
I am a fast learner.
Learning is fun and exciting.
I read write and learn very quickly.
I have many gifts and talents.
I make wise decisions.
I enjoy eating healthy foods.
I am destined to live a life of prosperity.
My thoughts create my world.
All is well in my world.
I think positive thus creating a positive world.
My positive attitude attracts positive situations and positive circumstances.
What I think about often eventually becomes my reality.
I attract situations that matches how I feel.
I visualize what I want often.
I talk about what I want often.
I think about what I want often.
I am a kind and generous person.

I show compassion towards others.
I treat people how I want to be treated.
What I do to others I actually do myself.
I take my schoolwork very seriously.
I am dedicated to being a wonderful student.
There isn't anything that I cannot be do or have.
I excel in my academics.
I am a natural born leader.
I am strong fit and athletic.
My mind is powerful and I use it wisely.
I am safe.
I am loved.
I am friendly.
I am brave.
I am courageous.
I am a winner.
I am very creative.
I believe in myself.
I trust my abilities.
I am confident.
I make friends easily.
I am a good person.
I am a good friend.
I always overcome my challenges.
I believe in my abilities.
I listen to my inner wisdom.
I am tough and durable.

I can do anything.
I am completely unlimited.
I only think about the things I want to happen.
I am honest.
I am forgiving.
I am trustworthy.
I am very responsible.
I take care of my responsibilities.
I am wealthy.
I am prosperous.
I am abundant.
I am divinely protected.
I think big.
I believe in myself and my abilities.
I am extremely confident.

I have the courage to by myself.
I love me.
I am a bright student.
I value my education.
Obtaining knowledge is very important to me.
I love and value my family.
I go after what I want and I accomplish my goals.
I am a go getter.

My thoughts are very powerful and I choose them carefully.
I am safe.
I am loved.
I am friendly.
I am brave.

61 minutes

CONCLUSION

Thank you so much for listening to *Kids Bedtime Sleep Meditations.*

I hope this book has helped you have lots of wonderful dreams and amazing nights of sleep.

If you ever find yourself stressed out, angry, overwhelmed or sad, you can always refer to this book's teachings and re-listen to it again.

If you enjoyed this book and if it has helped you have a better night's sleep, be sure to leave a thoughtful review on Amazon of how this book has helped you. This is so more kids like you can have amazing sleeps every night!

Thank you again for listening to this book and I wish you all the love, happiness and amazing nights of sleep ahead!